## Illustrated by Lesley Blackman

ISBN 0 86112 818 4

# Learn with Elephant

TED SMART

# The Elephant's Counting Book

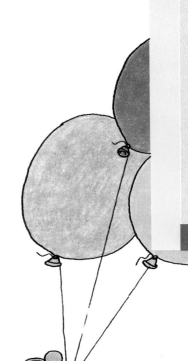

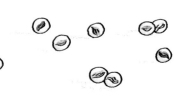

# 1

one

# 3

three

# 5

five

# 7

seven

# 11

eleven

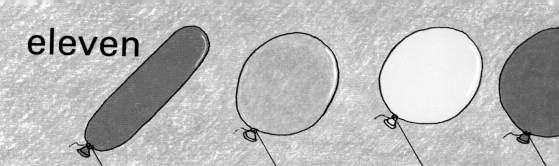

**12** twelve

thirteen

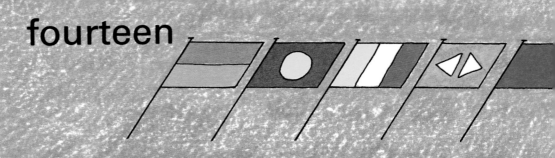

**15**

fifteen

sixteen

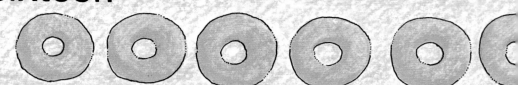

# 17

seventeen

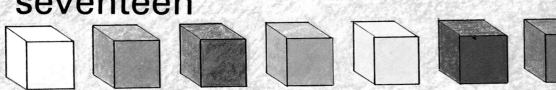

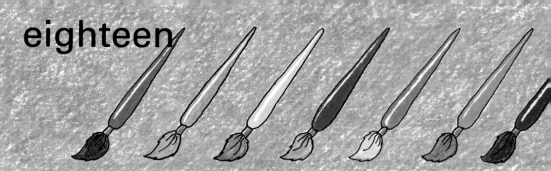

# 19

nineteen

twenty

# Elephant's birthday party

1

2

3

4

5

**6**

**7**

**8**

**9**

**10**

# Shopping with Elephant

**1**

**2**

**3**

**4**

**5**

# Elephant's Christmas

1

2

3

4

5

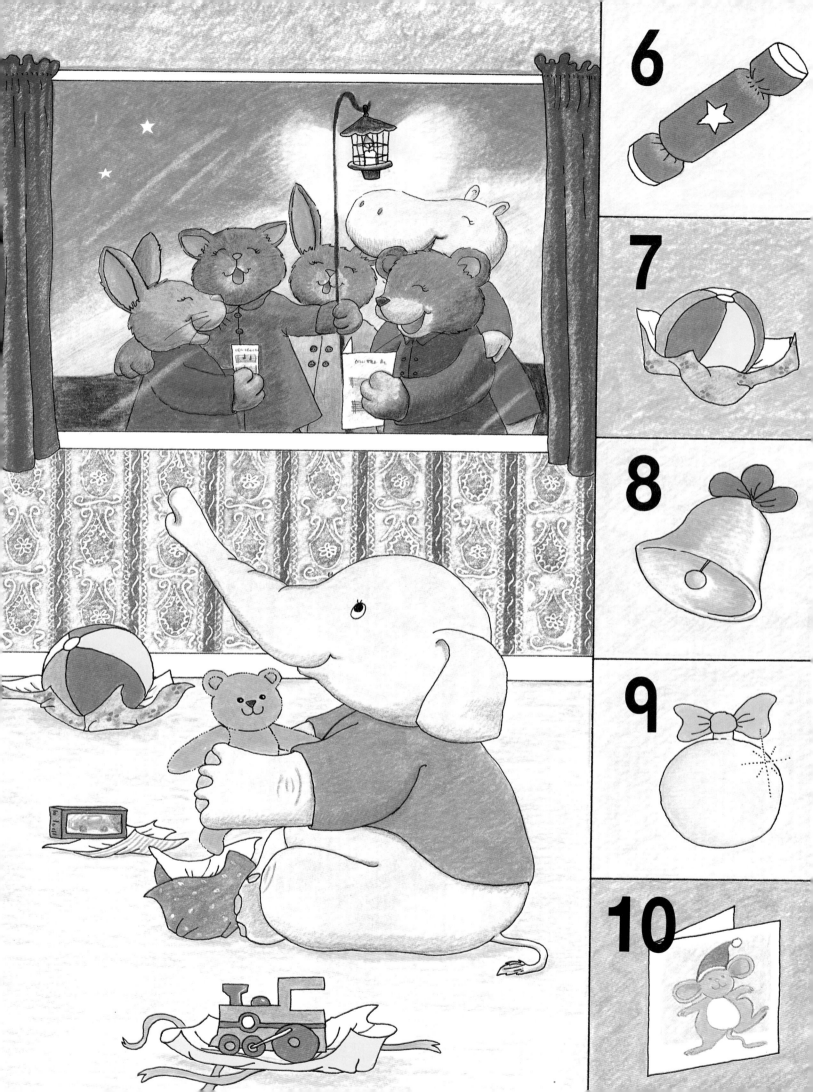

**6**

**7**

**8**

**9**

**10**

# Counting songs

One, two, buckle my shoe
Three, four, knock at the door
Five, six, pick up sticks
Seven, eight, lay them straight
Nine, ten, big fat hen

1   2

3   4

5   6

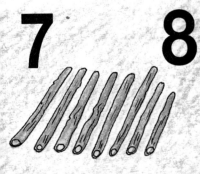

7   8

9   10

One, two, three, four, five
Once I caught a fish alive.
Six, seven, eight, nine, ten
Then I let it go again.

Why did you let it go?
Because it bit my finger so.
Which finger did it bite?
This little finger on the right.

# The Elephant's Alphabet

# A B C D E F G H I J K L M
## a b c d e f g h i j k l n

acorns ant ape

accordion alligator apple

# NOPQRSTUVWXYZ
# nopqrstuvwxyz

ark

anchor

arch

arrow

How many more things can you see beginning with Aa?

# A B C D E F G H I J K L M
## a b c d e f g h i j k l n

bear      bicycle      book

banana      bracelet      blanket

N O P Q R S T U V W X Y Z
n o p q r s t u v w x y z

box

bun

bottles

bush

Find all the things
that are blue.

A B C D E F G H I J K L M
a b c d e f g h i j k l n

cake          candle          chair

clock         carrots         cherries

**cabbage**

**chimpanzee**

**How many things can you find beginning with Cc?**

# A B C D E F G H I J K L M
## a b c d e f g h i j k l m

daffodils   desk   dice

dragon fly   diamond   dog

NOPQRSTUVWXYZ

nopqrstuvwxyz

daisies     deer

dragon      drink

How many animals
are there beginning
with Dd?

# A B C D E F G H I J K L M
## a b c d e f g h i j k l m

ear

eagle

emu

earrings

envelopes

earphones

# N O P Q R S T U V W X Y Z
## n o p q r s t u v w x y z

elephant      easel

Easter cards

How many Easter eggs can you find?

# A B C D E F G H I J K L M
## a b c d e f g h i j k l n

fence      fan      flies

flamingo      fish      foxglove

# N O P Q R S T U V W X Y Z
# n o p q r s t u v w x y z

fox

frog

flowers

fruit

What else can you see that starts with Ff?

# A B C D E F G H I J K L M
## a b c d e f g h i j k l m

gate      glass      gnome

garden      giraffe      gloves

N O P Q R S T U V W X Y Z
n o p q r s t u v w x y z

goat          goose

golf club     grapes

Find all the
things that
are green.

# A B C D E F G H I J K L M
## a b c d e f g h i j k l m

hand       hat

hot dog    handkerchief

# N O P Q R S T U V W X Y Z
# n o p q r s t u v w x y z

hoop            horses

hippopotamus

Find more things
starting with Hh.

# A B C D E F G H I J K L M
## a b c d e f g h i j k l r

igloo    icecream    ice

ice cubes    ice skates    ice berg

jug        jacket

juggle

How many more things beginning with Ii and Jj are there?

# A B C D E F G H I J K L M
## a b c d e f g h i j k l r

key        kite        knife

kangaroo    kingfisher    kitten

N O P Q R S T U V W X Y Z
n o p q r s t u v w x y z

**knees**     **knot**

**knitting**     **koala**

Find more things
beginning with Kk.

# A B C D E F G H I J K L M
# a b c d e f g h i j k l m

laces

leaves

leek

lemon

loaf

lettuce

# O P Q R S T U V W X Y Z
# o p q r s t u v w x y z

list

ladder

letter

leopard

There are lots more things to find starting with Ll.

# A B C D E F G H I J K L M

## a b c d e f g h i j k l m

magician     mirror     mole

magic wand     milkshake     mouse

# O P Q R S T U V W X Y Z
# o p q r s t u v w x y z

money      moose

monkey    mittens

Are there any more magical things starting with Mm?

# A B C D E F G H I J K L M
## a b c d e f g h i j k l m

**newspaper**  **nightcap**  **nest**

**night shirt**  **noteboard**  **nuts**

# OPQRSTUVWXYZ
## opqrstuvwxyz

necklace    nail

notebook    notes

How many more
things starting
with Nn are there?

# A B C D E F G H I J K L M
## a b c d e f g h i j k l r

orange    opera    oboe

orchestra    organ    octopus

# O P Q R S T U V W X Y Z
# o p q r s t u v w x y z

otter       owl

oak tree    ostrich

Find all the
things beginning
with Oo.

# A B C D E F G H I J K L M
# a b c d e f g h i j k l r

paper      perch      pelican

paints      parrot      penguin

pig          plate

pink         plums

How many more
things are there
beginning with Pp?

# ABCDEFGHIJKL
## abcdefghijkl

question mark quilt quill

rocking chair race rafts

radio river

rhinoceros rainbow

Can you find
the robin?

# A B C D E F G H I J K L M
## a b c d e f g h i j k l n

sand        sea        ship

sandcastle    seagull    squirrel

shells      sock

sandwich      shoes

How many
shells are there?

# A B C D E F G H I J K L M
## a b c d e f g h i j k l m

telephone  tiger  track

teddy bear  train  trees

# N O P Q R S T U V W X Y Z
# n o p q r s t u v w x y z

tunnel  vase

umbrella  violets

What other toys are there?

# A B C D E F G H I J K L M
# a b c d e f g h i j k l m

wizard       wand       watch

waitress    walrus    woodpecke

# OPQRSTUVWXYZ
# opqrstuvwxyz

wig

wigwam

windmill

warpaint

What else
starts with Ww?

# A B C D E F G H I J K L M
## a b c d e f g h i j k l m

box            fox            yellow

xylophone      yacht          yogurt

N O P Q R S T U V W X Y Z

n o p q r s t u v w x y z

yo-yo          zodiac

zebra          zig-zag          How many
things are yellow?

# The Elephant's Wordbook

balloon

clown

# Aa

acorn

angel

apple

ant

apricot

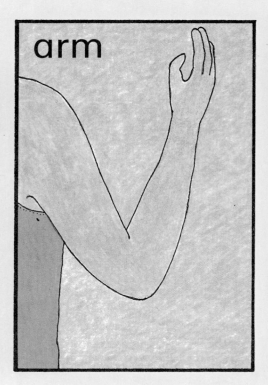

arm

apron

A a  B b  C c  D d  E e  F f  G g
H h  I i  J j  K k  L l  M m  N n
O o  P p  Q q  R r  S s  T t
U u  V v  W w  X x  Y y  Z z

alphabet

# B b

bridge

bear

book

boat

butterfly

bed

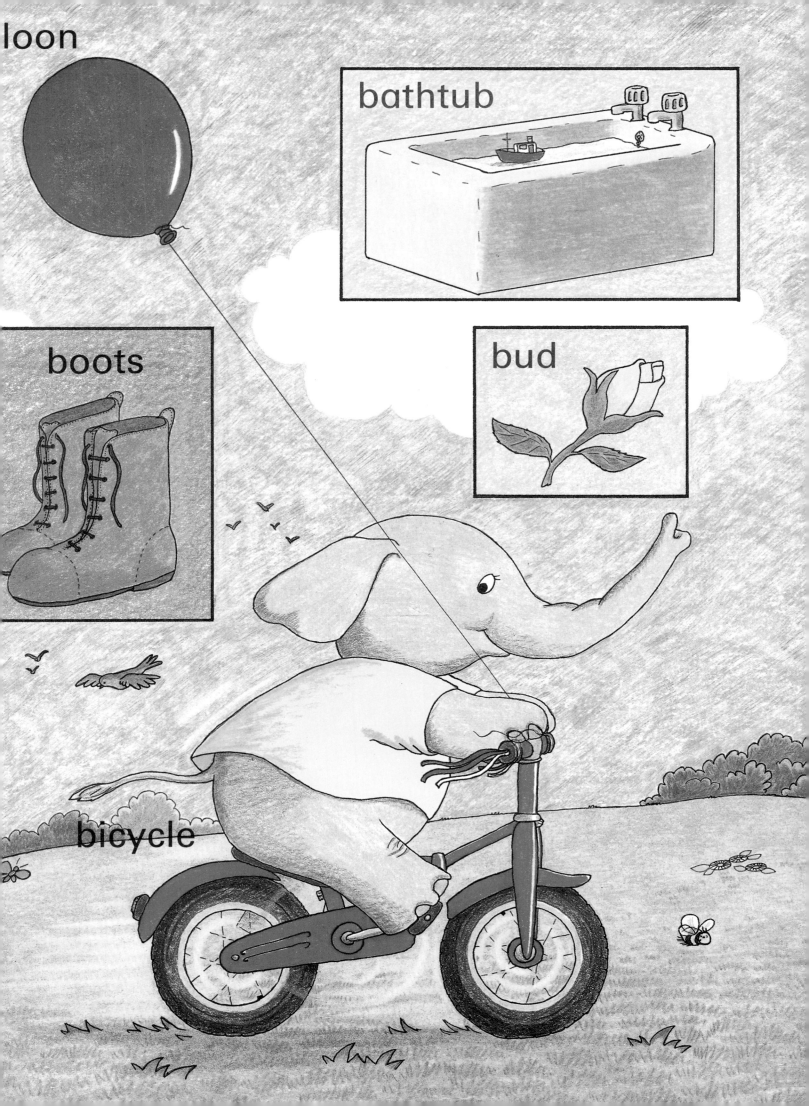

loon

bathtub

bud

boots

bicycle

# Cc

cake

castle

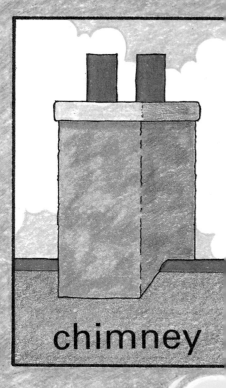
chimney

ca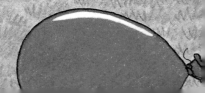

clock

cow

crayon

crab

circus

clown

# Dd

dinosaur

doll

dress

daffodil

duck

dog

dwarf

donkey

# E e

egg

elephant

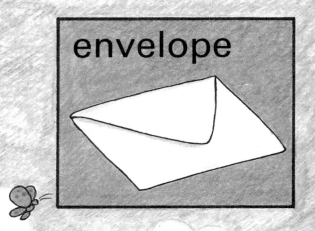

envelope

engine

# F f

fan

feather

fish

flower

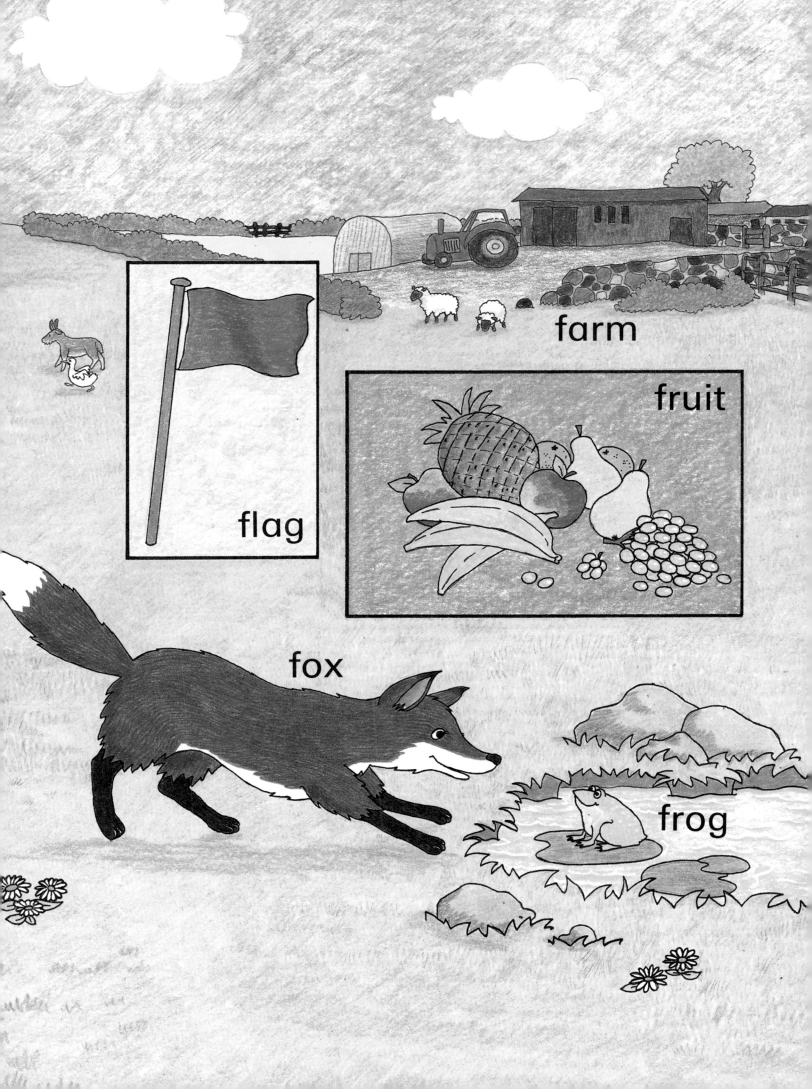

farm

flag

fruit

fox

frog

# Gg

garage

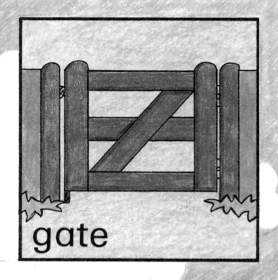

gate

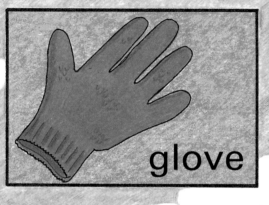

glove

goat

goose

giraffe

ghost

guitar

gorilla

# Hh

hammer

hat

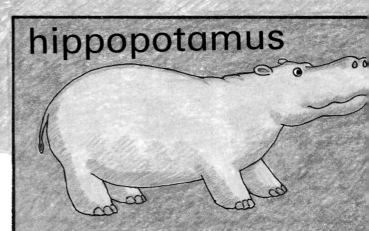
hippopotamus

honey

HONEY

hummingbird

helicopter

horse

house

# Ii Jj

juggler

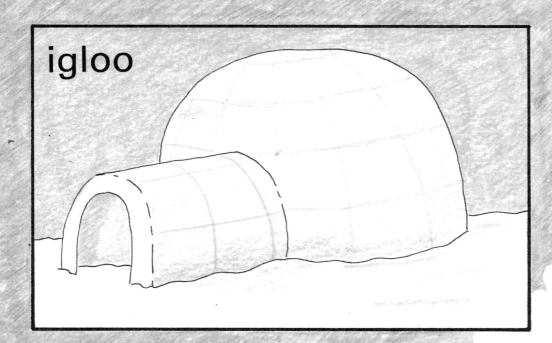
igloo

ink

jack
-in-the-box

insect

ice cream

jug

# K k

koala

king

key

# L l

lemon

ladder

lamb

eopard

lion

lettuce

# M m

medal

map

mirror

mouse

mushroom

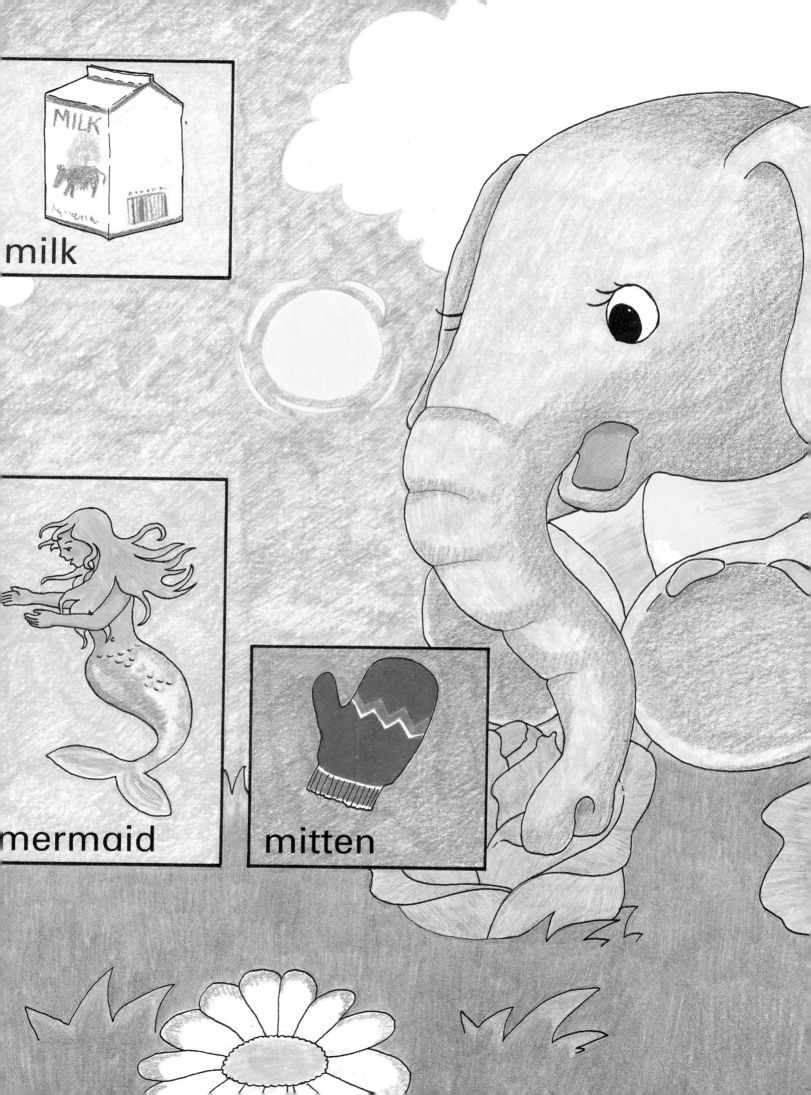

milk

mermaid

mitten

# Nn

newspaper

necklace

nut

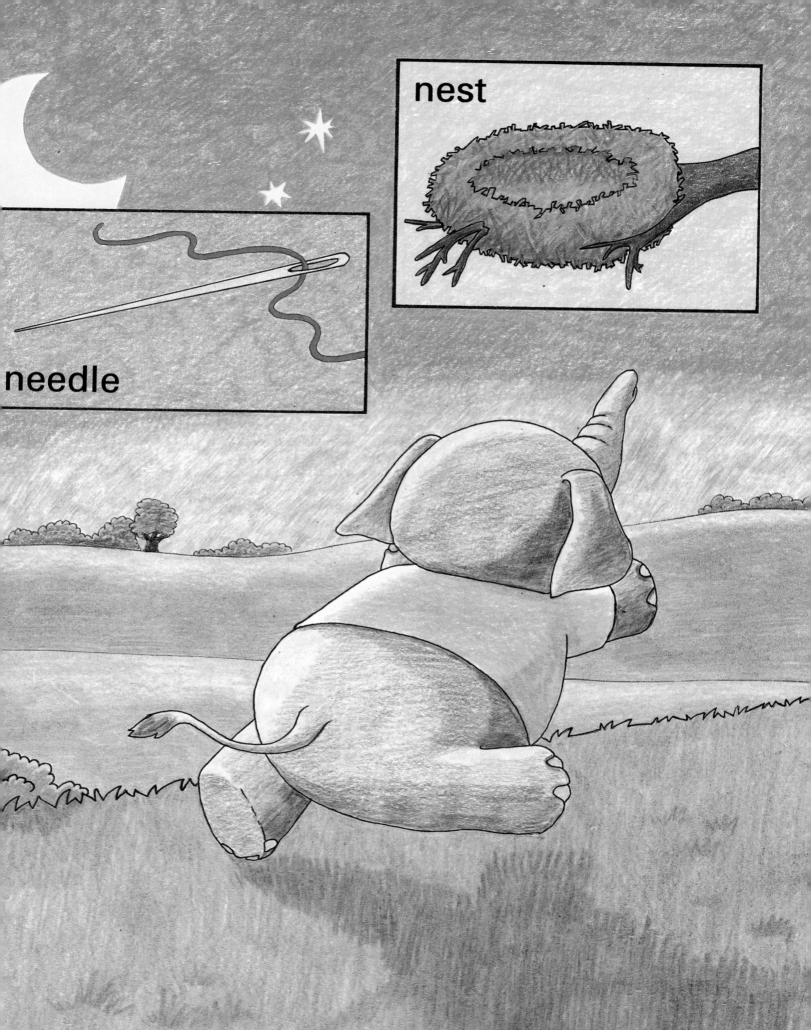

nest

needle

# Oo

onion

owl

octopus

ostrich

otter

orange

# Pp

parachute

paint

panda

plane

peacock

pig

plate

pirate

# Qq Rr

queen

rainbow

rabbit

quilt

rocket

reindeer

rocking chair

robot

# S s

seal

sandcastle

snowman

squirrel

socks

sun

spider

scarf

scooter

# T t U u V v

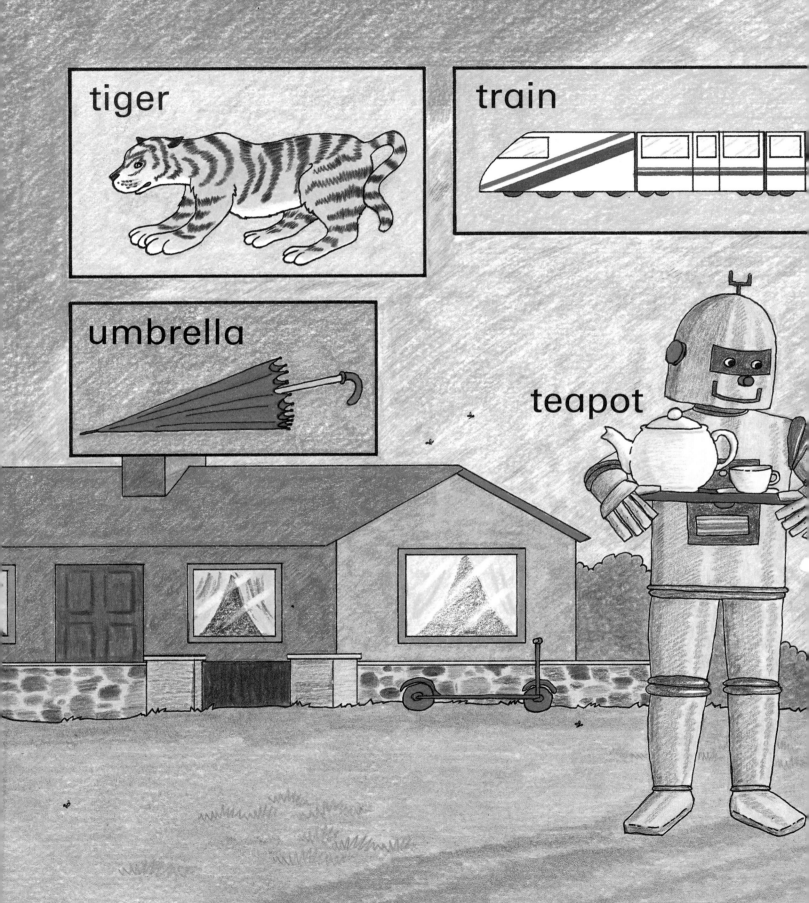

tiger

train

umbrella

teapot

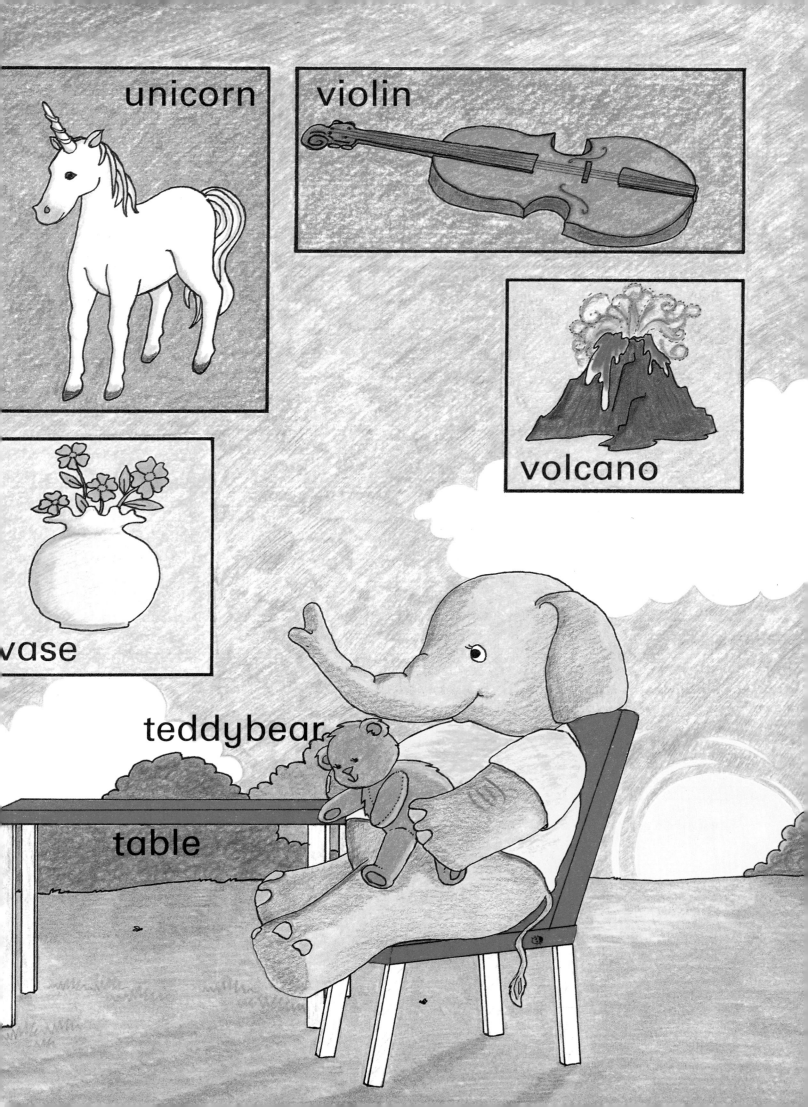

unicorn

violin

volcano

vase

teddybear

table

# W w

window

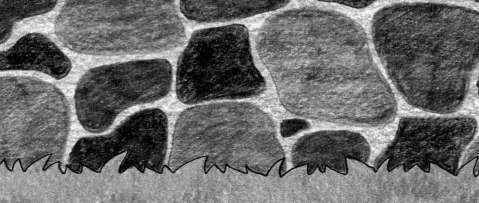
walrus

waterfall

windmill

well

whale

witch

wheelbarrow

wall

# Xx Yy Zz

yak

fox

zipper

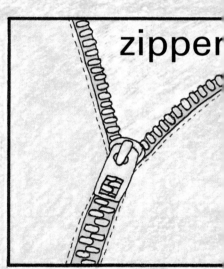

box

xylophone

yacht

yo-yo

zebra

# The Elephant's Find and Say

# On the Beach

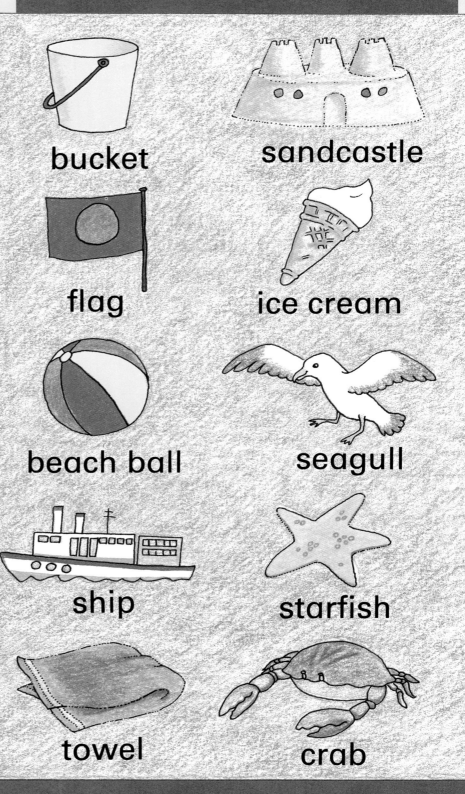

bucket

sandcastle

flag

ice cream

beach ball

seagull

ship

starfish

towel

crab

How many shells
can you find?

# In the Park

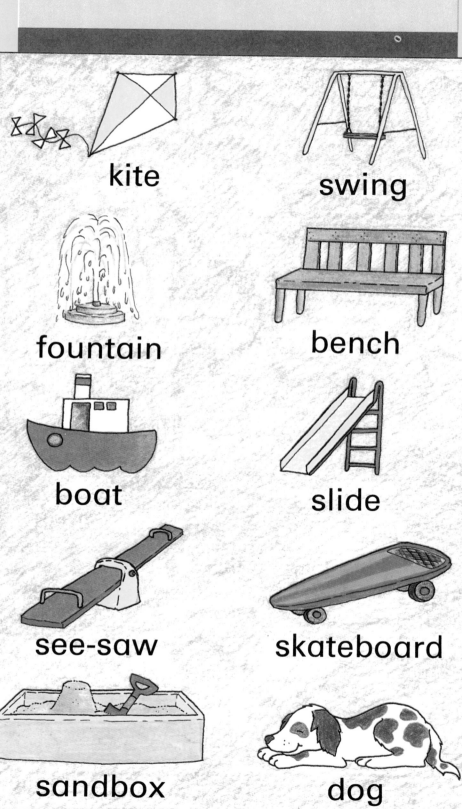

kite

swing

fountain

bench

boat

slide

see-saw

skateboard

sandbox

dog

Where is the boat?

# At the Circus

juggler

acrobat

clown

tightrope

trapeze

ringmaster

popcorn

ring

stilts

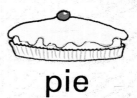
pie

Who is throwing the custard pie?

# In the Garden

watering can

sprinkler

cabbage

flowerpot

flower

wheelbarrow

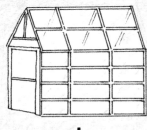
greenhouse

carrot

shed

bush

**What is Elephant planting?**

# Playing Games

tennis racquet

yo-yo

hoop

marbles

dominoes

hopscotch

roller skates

basket ball

shuttlecock

bicycle

How many balls are there?

# The Animals' Fancy Dress

fan

crown

tray

lasso

parrot

shield

helmet

feather

bandage

wand

Who is dressed as a king?

# A Visit to the Toyshop

jack-in-the-box

doll

teddy bear

train

jig-saw puzzle

car

drum

book

plane

blocks

How many blocks are there?

# Playing in a Band

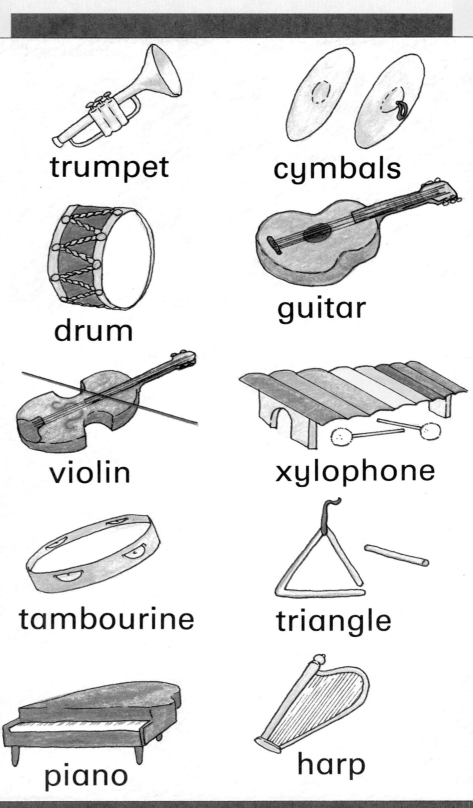

trumpet

cymbals

drum

guitar

violin

xylophone

tambourine

triangle

piano

harp

How do you play the different instruments?

# Cooking in the Kitchen

stove

rolling pin

flour

apron

butter

frying pan

mixing bowl

wooden spoon

eggs

table

How many blue cups
can you see?

# Happy Birthday, Elephant

cake

candle

balloon

present

straw

party hat

camera

blindfold

cookie

sandwich

How old is Elephant?

# A Rainy Day

puddle

umbrella

boots

raincoat

rainbow

rain hat

frog

boat

bridge

cloud

Who is jumping in the puddles?

# Working Outside

hammer

window

toolbox

hammock

nail

garage

paint

broom

fence

car

How many windows are there?

# On the Farm

tractor

pig

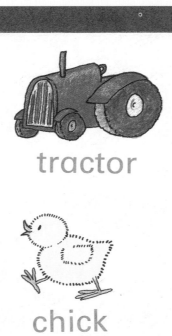

chick

horse

goat

scarecrow

lamb

cow

duck

pond

What noises do the animals make?

# Fruit Picking

basket

pear

strawberry

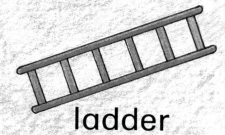

ladder

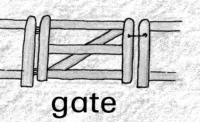

gate

raspberry

plum

apple

tree

squirrel

How many baskets are there?

# At the Shops

sweater

shoes

jeans

bag

shirt

socks

money

cap

tie

skirt

**What is Elephant buying?**

# Out in the Snow

ice skates

snowman

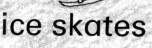
skis

gloves

scarf

toboggan

snowballs

robin

icicles

hat

Who is skating?

# Down by the River

fish

jar

rabbit

tadpole

bees

fishing rod

windmill

net

caterpillar

butterfly

How many bees are there?

paint brushes

easel

picture

blackboard

scissors

paints

pencils

clock

chalk

paper

What is Elephant painting?

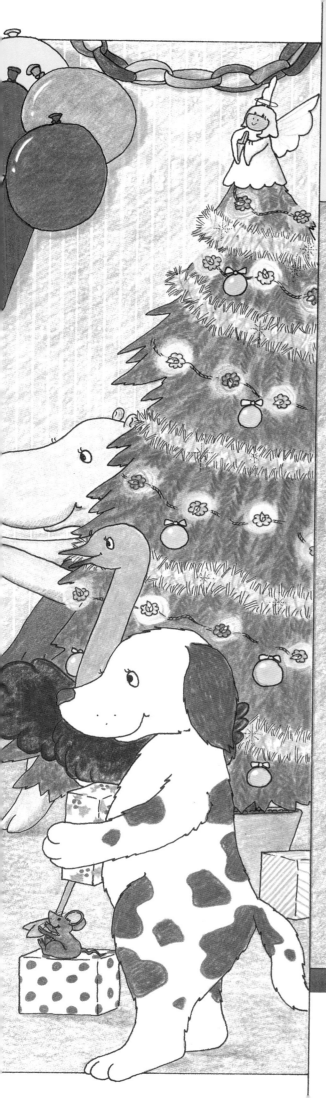

# Christmas Time

Christmas tree

holly

lights

presents

tinsel

stocking

card

mistletoe

carol singer

angel

Who is dressed as
Santa Claus?

# Time for Bed

stars

slippers

comb

mirror

pillow

bed

bathtub

toothbrush

soap

sponge

What time does Elephant go to bed?